Mighty Mammals

WELDON OWEN PTY LTD

Chairman: John Owen
Publisher: Sheena Coupe
Associate Publisher: Lynn Humphries
Managing Editor: Helen Bateman
Design Concept: Sue Rawkins
Senior Designer: Kylie Mulquin
Production Manager: Caroline Webber
Production Assistant: Kylie Lawson

Text: Sharon Dalgleish
Consultant: George McKay, Conservation Biologist
U.S. Editors: Laura Cavaluzzo and Rebecca McEwen

04 03 02 01 00 99
10 9 8 7 6 5 4 3 2 1

Published in the United States by
Shortland Publications, Inc.
P.O. Box 6195
Denver, CO 80206-0195

Printed in Australia.
ISBN: 0-7699-0478-5

CONTENTS

INTRODUCING MAMMALS

Dogs, cats, and most of the other animals we keep as pets are mammals, and we humans are mammals, too. Mammals are warm-blooded—their body temperature stays the same no matter how hot or cold it is. All mammals feed their young milk and most give birth to live young.

Ears and Noses
The African aardvark has a large nose and big ears. Like many mammals, it has a good sense of smell and good hearing.

Sleeping Over

Food is scarce in winter, so many mammals save energy by sleeping for long periods. While they sleep, they live off the fat stored in their bodies. This is called hibernation.

Family Life

Lions are typical mammals, which feed their young with milk.

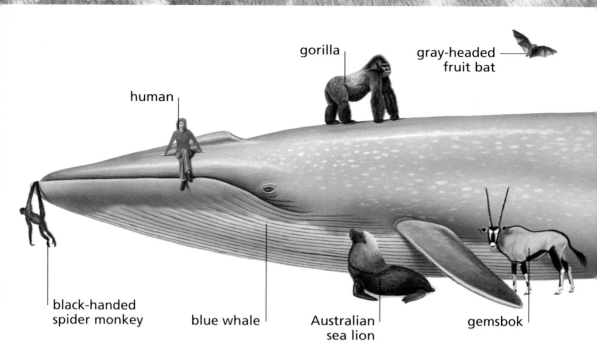

gorilla

gray-headed fruit bat

human

black-handed spider monkey

blue whale

Australian sea lion

gemsbok

ALL SHAPES AND SIZES

Mammals can survive in most environments because they are warm-blooded. They can live in jungles, deserts, and high mountains; in the air and in the trees. They can live in the polar regions and in the oceans, and even beneath the ground. Different mammals have different body shapes to suit the way they live.

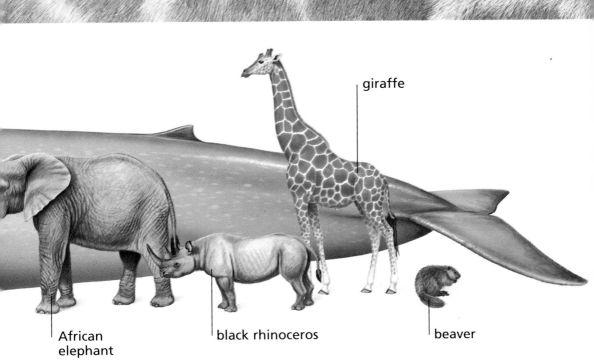

giraffe

African
elephant

black rhinoceros

beaver

Looking Alike

Some mammals look like each other even though they live in different parts of the world. Australian koalas look and behave like the sloths of Central and South America. Echidnas look like the pangolins of Africa and Asia.

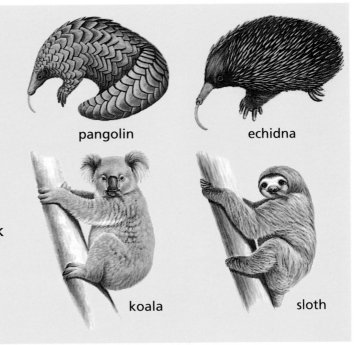

pangolin

echidna

koala

sloth

Fringe Filter
Baleen whales have long fringes of baleen instead of teeth. They eat by filtering food through the fringes.

WHAT'S FOR DINNER?

Some mammals are hunters. Some are scavengers and eat leftovers. Others are fussy about what they eat. Echidnas like to eat ants, while vampire bats live on blood. Baleen whales eat tiny shrimp called krill and plankton. The giraffe gazelle lives in the desert and eats leaves that contain water. It never needs to drink!

During the day, hyenas are scavengers. They eat the remains of animals killed by lions. At night they hunt prey themselves.

ELEPHANTS

Elephants are the largest animals living on land. They love baths—even mud baths! By coating themselves with mud and dust, they protect their skin from sunburn. To keep cool, they spend several hours each day in the water, sucking water into their trunks and showering it over their body. An elephant's trunk can pick up a single twig or pull a whole tree out of the ground.

Family Ties
Elephant families are very caring. A baby elephant has many aunts who help look after it.

Elephants live in family groups made up of only females and their young. The oldest female is the leader. The male elephant, called the bull, lives alone, away from the herd.

BEARS

Different sorts of bears are adapted to different environments and to eating different foods. Sloth bears eat termites. They make a tube with their lips and suck the termites through a gap in their teeth. Polar bears are the largest meat-eating animals on land. They eat mainly seals, but have also been known to catch small whales. Grizzly bears eat berries, plant roots, fish, grubs, honey, and even moths, as well as meat.

DID YOU KNOW?

A polar bear's fur looks white against the snow, but it's really made up of clear, hollow hairs that trap heat. Polar bears have fur on the bottom of their paws, which is why they can run on snow and ice—they have their own snowshoes!

Sleeping In

Grizzly bears hibernate for up to six months each year, sleeping inside their cozy dens while it is snowing and cold outside. Most dens are dug under large trees.

Sun Bear

The smallest bear is the sun bear. It licks honey from beehives with its long tongue.

WHALES

The blue whale is the largest mammal that has ever lived. An adult weighs the same as about 1,300 adult men! Whales live in the sea, but they have to come to the surface, where they breathe through a blowhole on the top of their head. Sperm whales and dolphins are toothed whales. Humpback whales (shown at right) are baleen whales. They strain their food through hairlike plates called baleen.

Killer Whales
Killer whales, or orcas, are clever hunters. They eat fish, squid, penguins, seals, and sea lions. Sometimes they kill other whales and porpoises.

Champion Divers

A sperm whale can dive up to 2,187 yards (2,000 meters)—that's deeper than any other mammal can dive.

Useful Tusks

A male walrus's tusks can grow to more than a yard long. Walruses use them to help pull themselves out of the water onto ice.

Seals and Walruses

Earless seals are good swimmers, but on land they have to crawl like caterpillars! Sea lions, or eared seals, can turn their back flippers forward to walk on land. These Australian sea lions are hunting squid and fish. Baby sea lions learn to swim when they are about one month old.

Amazing!

Sea lions live in noisy groups called colonies. One colony can have thousands of animals. Males fight each other to breed with females, then they guard them in groups called harems.

Kangaroos

Most kangaroos and wallabies live in family groups. In the breeding season, pairs of males have boxing matches, kicking and punching each other until one is defeated. If they want to move quickly, kangaroos hop in giant bounds. To move more slowly, they balance on their tail and front legs while they bring their back legs forward.

Take a Seat
The forest wallaby of New Guinea bends its tail as a prop when it sits.

Warm and Safe

A baby kangaroo spends
many months in its mother's
pouch, warm and protected,
until it's ready to survive
on its own.

Swingers

Orangutans move around in trees by dangling by their arms and swinging hand-over-hand.

APES

Try moving the thumb of one hand to touch each of the fingers on the same hand. An ape can do that, too! Like you, apes have flattened fingernails and no tail. Orangutans, chimpanzees, and gorillas are all apes. Orangutans live in trees most of the time. Chimpanzees and gorillas live mainly on the ground. They walk on all fours, supporting their arms on their knuckles.

GORILLAS

DID YOU KNOW?

Chimpanzees build a bed for the night by bending and breaking tree branches. The next night they build another bed in another tree.

MAMMALS WITH HOOVES

Many scientists believe that about 40 million years ago, plant-eating mammals began to live on open grasslands. The only way they could escape predators was to run. They ran faster on their toes than with a flatter foot, so over millions of years, their toes slowly turned into hard hooves. The toes that were not needed for support grew smaller or disappeared.

DID YOU KNOW?

An elephant still has all of its toes. It has five toes on each of its front feet, covered by a tough, hooflike casing of skin.

Walking under Water

Hippos have to stay in the water during the day, so their sensitive skin doesn't dry out. They have long, wide toes for walking on the bottom of lakes.

On Tippy Toes

How many toes does each of these mammals have?

WILDEBEEST

Wildebeest live on the vast Serengeti plains of eastern Africa, grazing on tall grasses. Each year, at the end of the rainy season, hundreds of herds of wildebeest migrate up to 1,864 miles (3,000 kilometers) in a huge circle. A herd might have 10,000 animals searching for water and grass.

Baby Boom

Wildebeests time the birth of their babies to make sure a large number are born at one time. This spreads the risk from predators.

RHINOCEROSES

Rhinoceroses are related to horses, but these massive plant-eating animals weigh nearly 3 tons (3.2 tonnes) and have short, thick legs to support them. The white rhino and the Indian rhino eat mainly grass, while the other rhinos browse on leaves. People have killed so many rhinos for their horns that all species are endangered.

Rare Rhinos
Today, there are only five species of rhinos in the world. More than 50 species are extinct.

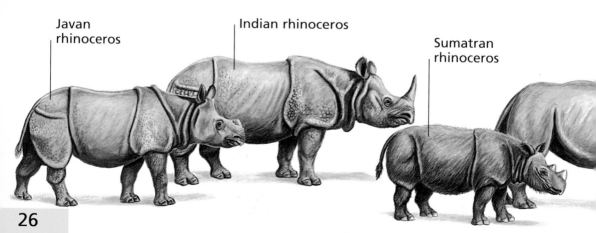

Javan rhinoceros

Indian rhinoceros

Sumatran rhinoceros

BLACK RHINO

white
rhinoceros

black
rhinoceros

THE CAT FAMILY

All cats are good hunters. They stalk their prey silently and then attack in a sudden rush. When they have their prey on the ground, they kill it with a bite to the throat or neck. Many species of cats are endangered. They have been hunted for their skins, and have had their wild habitats taken over by humans.

Great Cats
Tigers are the largest living cats. A Siberian tiger can grow to 4 yards (3.7 meters) long and can weigh more than 700 pounds (320 kilograms).

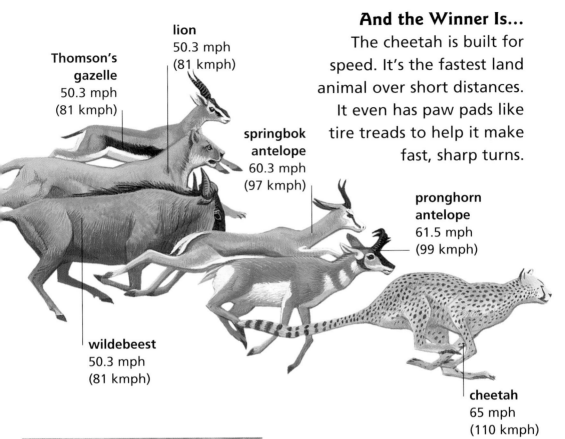

Thomson's
gazelle
50.3 mph
(81 kmph)

lion
50.3 mph
(81 kmph)

springbok
antelope
60.3 mph
(97 kmph)

And the Winner Is...
The cheetah is built for speed. It's the fastest land animal over short distances. It even has paw pads like tire treads to help it make fast, sharp turns.

pronghorn
antelope
61.5 mph
(99 kmph)

wildebeest
50.3 mph
(81 kmph)

cheetah
65 mph
(110 kmph)

DID YOU KNOW?

Lions live in a family group called a pride. Female lions do most of the hunting, but the male lion always eats first when the females bring back the prey! When he's full, the females and cubs can eat.

GLOSSARY

adapted A description of a plant or animal that has changed its behavior or body to allow it to survive in new conditions.

endangered In danger of becoming extinct.

habitat The home of a plant or animal.

hibernate To have a long period of very deep sleep.

migration The traveling animals do from one habitat or climate to another at specific times of the year.

predators Animals that hunt and kill other animals.

prey Animals that are caught and eaten by other animals.

scavenger An animal that eats the remains of prey killed by predators.

tusks Very long teeth that grow out of the mouth of walruses, elephants, and some other animals.

warm-blooded A description for an animal whose body temperature stays the same, no matter what the temperature is outside the animal's body.

INDEX

CREDITS AND NOTES

Picture and Illustration Credits
[t=top, b=bottom, l=left, r=right, c=center, F=front, B=back, C=cover, bg=background]
Auscape/Jean-Marc La Roque 14–15rc. **Auscape/Doug Perrine** 15tr. **Andre Boos** 9cr. **Martin Camm** 10–11cr. **Corel Corporation** 11tl, 12bl, 19tr, 23tr, 29bl. **Simone End** 1c, 3tr, 4bl, 5tr, 13tr, 16tl, 16–17lc, 17br, 30bc. **Christer Eriksson** 4–5cr, 18–19c. **Jon Gittoes** 20tr. **Tim Hayward/Bernard Thornton Artists UK** 8tl, 8–9c. **David Kirshner** 6–7tc, 7bc, 7br, 7rc, 7c, 12–13br, 18bl, 26bl, 26br, 26bc, 26–27cr, 27bl, 27r, 31tr. **Frank Knight** 2l, 10bl, 13tl, 22bl, 22cr, 22–23c, 23lc, 23br, 28bl, 29tc, FCrc. **PhotoDisc** 4–32 borders, Cbg. **Tony Pyrzakowski** 14bl, BC. **Barbara Rodanska** 21cr, 25tr. **Trevor Ruth** 24–25c. **Peter Schouten** 20–21lc, FCbc.

Acknowledgements
Weldon Owen would like to thank the following people for their assistance in the production of this book:
Jocelyne Best, Ivan Finnegan, Peta Gorman, Tracey Jackson, Andrew Kelly, Sarah Mattern, Emily Wood.